MW00559256

EVERYBODY'S
POPULAR MUSIC
FOR GUITAR

1

A COLLECTION OF THE
VERY BEST POPULAR MUSIC

Philip Groeber, David Hoge

Production: Frank J. Hackinson

Production Coordinator: Philip Groeber

Cover Design: Terpstra Design, San Francisco

Text Editor: Pamela Hoge

Engraving: Tempo Music Press, Inc.

Printer: Tempo Music Press, Inc.

THE
F·J·H
MUSIC
COMPANY
IN C.

Frank J. Hackinson

ISBN-13: 978-1-56939-767-1

HOW TO USE THIS BOOK

Everybody's Popular Music For Guitar offers favorite popular songs for all ages. Popular music can present challenges to beginning students due to extended melodies and more complex rhythms. However, the music in this book has been carefully arranged for beginning guitarists of all ages.

This book is correlated to **Everybody's Guitar Method Book 1**, and may also be used as a supplement to any other guitar method.

Each arrangement includes melody, chord names, and lyrics, and is readily adaptable for ensemble playing. The student is encouraged to learn both the melody and the chords whenever possible.

This book contains many popular, rock, jazz, and classical music standards, all of which will be important additions to your repertoire. Have fun playing these songs for yourself and others.

Other features include:

 The pros offer their insight on how to practice effectively. Important music terms are in **bold** print.

 These provide historical facts and important information relating to the music.

- **Natural Notes in First Position** and **Chords Used in This Book** — reference charts to help students play melodies and/or strum chords to their favorite popular songs. (page 34–35)

- **Everybody's Popular Guitar Riffs** — a sneak peek to what is to appear in **Everybody's Popular Music for Guitar 2**. (page 34)

- **Glossary** — a quick reference for terms used throughout the book. (page 36)

G1044

CONTENTS

Music

Supplementary Material

Bugler's Dream
(Olympic Fanfare)

Leo Arnaud

*Synchronize the motions of your right and left hands to help produce a **legato** (smooth, connected notes) sound.*

Always count and play evenly when practicing new music.
Make sure to hold each note for its full rhythmic value.

Quarter note (♩) = 1 beat   **Half note** (♪) = 2 beats
Dotted half note (♩.) = 3 beats   **Whole note** (o) = 4 beats

Dynamics are symbols that indicate how loudly or softly to play music.
The most common dynamics are:

p (*piano*) = soft   *mp* (*mezzo piano*) = medium soft

f (*forte*) = loud   *mf* (*mezzo forte*) = medium loud

G1044

The Lion Sleeps Tonight
from Walt Disney's *The Lion King*

Music and Lyrics by
George David Weiss, Hugo Peretti,
Luigi Creatore and Solomon Linda

Note to teacher:

* Measures 17-25 may be taught by note
using swing rhythm (long-short note values).

G1044

Mrs. Robinson
from the movie *The Graduate*

Music and Lyrics by
Paul Simon

Left-hand fingering *is indicated by numbers (*1 *= index,* 2 *= middle,* 3 *= ring, and* 4 *= little). Follow the left-hand fingering carefully.*

A **rest** (𝄽) is a moment of silence in music. **Dampen** (mute) the strings with either the left or right hands to keep them from vibrating during a rest.

The **sharp** symbol (♯) *raises* the pitch of a note by one fret (one half step).

G1044

When the Saints Go Marching In

Traditional Spiritual

 music master

Pick-up notes are notes that come before the first complete measure. The beats in the pick-up measure and the last measure usually add up to one complete measure.

1st and 2nd endings — After playing music in the 1st ending bracket, repeat and then play the music in the 2nd ending bracket.

This Land Is Your Land

Music and Lyrics by
Woody Guthrie

This Land Is Your Land has been performed by Bob Dylan, The Kingston Trio, Bruce Springsteen, The Seekers, and Peter, Paul and Mary. It is one of the most popular American folk songs.

G1044

Heigh-Ho

from Walt Disney's *Snow White and the Seven Dwarfs*

Music by Frank Churchill
Lyrics by Larry Morey

The names of the seven dwarfs are Bashful, Doc, Dopey, Grumpy, Happy, Sleepy, and Sneezy.

Can You Feel the Love Tonight?

from Walt Disney's *The Lion King*

Music by Elton John
Lyrics by Tim Rice

G1044

Can You Feel the Love Tonight? won the Academy Award for Best Song in 1994. Elton John, the composer, won the Grammy Award for Best Male Pop Vocal Performance.

Chim Chim Cher-ee

from Walt Disney's *Mary Poppins*

Music and Lyrics by
Richard M. Sherman and Robert B. Sherman

G1044

21 Am   E+   Am7   D

Now   as   the   lad - der   of   life   'as   been   strung,   you

25 Dm   Am   B7

may   think   a   sweep's   on   the   bot - tom - most

28 E7   Am   E+

rung.   Though   I   spends   me   time   in   the

31 Am7   D   Dm

ash - es   and   smoke,   in   this   'ole   wide

34 Am   E7   Am

world   there's   no   'ap - pi - er   bloke,   in

37 Dm   Am   E7 *ritard.*   Am

this   'ole   wide   world   there's   no   'ap - pi - er   bloke.

*Learn the correct notes and rhythms before using **alternate picking** (⊓ ⋁ ⊓ ⋁) on eighth notes (⊓ = downstroke, ⋁ = upstroke). A good way to learn alternate picking is to begin with notes that are on the same string.*

A quarter note can be divided into two equal parts called **eighth notes**. A single eighth note has a flag (♪). Two or more eighth notes may be connected by a beam (♫). Be sure to keep a steady pulse when playing eighth notes.

♪ = ½ beat   ♫ = 1 beat   ♫♫ = 2 beats

Count: 1   +   1   +   2   +

Morning Mood

Edvard Grieg

Count: 1 + 2 + 3 +

Amazing Grace

Early American
Lyrics by John Newton

A - maz - ing Grace, how sweet the sound, that saved a wretch like me. I once was lost but now am found, was blind, but now, I see.

G1044

Reuben and Rachel

Music by William Gooch
Lyrics by Harry Birch

 Follow the left-hand fingering carefully for a legato sound (see measure 2).

 Reuben and Rachel was originally published in 1871, and has regained popularity as a children's song. This is a good song in which to be creative and write your own set of lyrics.

Rocky Top

Music and Lyrics by
Boudleaux Bryant and Felice Bryant

G1044

Ode to Joy
from *Symphony No. 9*

Ludwig van Beethoven

Exaggerate the dynamics.
Practice the new rhythm (measure 4) ♩ ♪♪ *slowly and carefully.*

Two distinctively different arrangements (*Ode to Joy* and *Joyful, Joyful*) of this famous melody were included in the sound track of *Sister Act 2: Back in the Habit*, starring Whoopi Goldberg.

G1044

Blowin' in the Wind

Music and Lyrics by
Bob Dylan

G1044

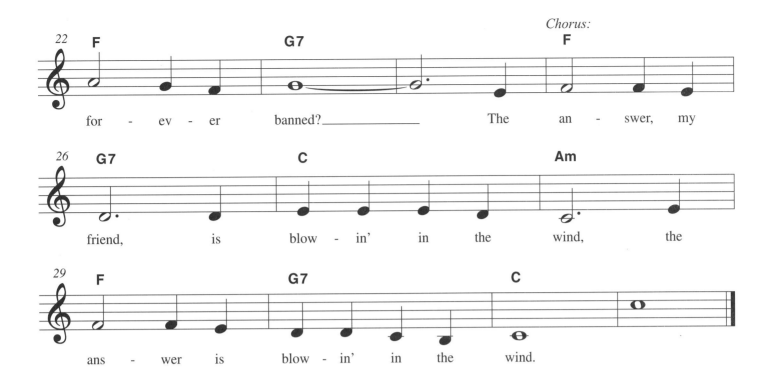

2. How many times must a man look up,
   Before he can see the sky?
   Yes, 'n' how many ears must one man have,
   Before he can hear people cry?
   Yes, 'n' how many deaths will it take till he knows,
   That too many people have died?

3. How many years can a mountain exist,
   Before it's washed to the sea?
   Yes, 'n' how many years can some people exist,
   Before they're allowed to be free?
   Yes, 'n' how many times can a man turn his head,
   Pretending he just doesn't see?

Blowin' in the Wind was released on the 1963 album *The Freewheelin' Bob Dylan*. The most commercially successful version of this song was recorded by the folk music trio Peter, Paul and Mary. Chet Atkins, Stan Getz, The Hollies, Dolly Parton, Elvis Presley, Stevie Wonder, and numerous other artists have also recorded this famous protest song.

Beautiful Dreamer

Music and Lyrics by
Stephen C. Foster

Stephen Foster (1826–1864) is known as the "father of American music."
A version of *Beautiful Dreamer* was performed in the 1986 movie
An American Tail.

G1044

song,_____   list   while   I   woo

thee   with   soft   mel   -   o   -   dy.

Verse:

Gone   are   the   cares   of   life's   bus   -   y

throng,_____   beau   -   ti   -   ful   dream   -   er,   a -

wake   un   -   to   me!_____

Beau   -   ti   -   ful   dream   -   er,   a   -   wake   un   -   to

me!   Let ring

In measures 52 through 54, hold your left-hand fingers down to allow the notes to ring. You will then be ready to play the C chord in the last measure.

Iron Man

Music and Lyrics by Frank Iommi, John Osbourne,
William Ward, and Terence Butler

G1044

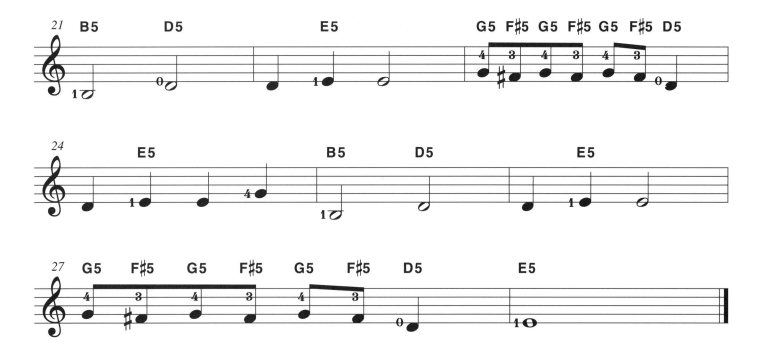

2. Is he live or dead? I see thoughts within his head.
   We'll just pass him there. Why should we even care?

3. Heavy boots of lead, fills his victims full of dread.
   Running as fast as they can. Iron Man lives again!

Carefully observe the left-hand fingering throughout. In measure 3, play the G note on the fourth string at the fifth fret.

When strumming power chords, use **guide fingers** *(keeping your left-hand fingers in contact with the strings) whenever possible. Use downstrokes (◼). In Iron Man, the root of the power chords is always on the fifth string.*

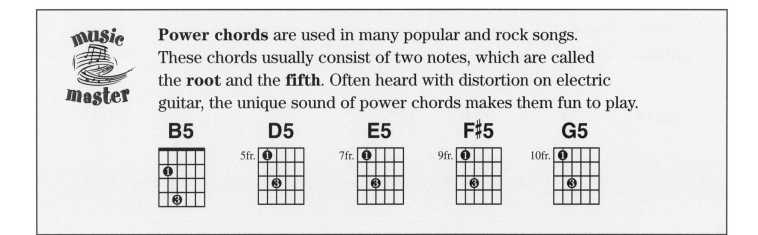

Power chords are used in many popular and rock songs. These chords usually consist of two notes, which are called the **root** and the **fifth**. Often heard with distortion on electric guitar, the unique sound of power chords makes them fun to play.

Worried Man Blues

Traditional

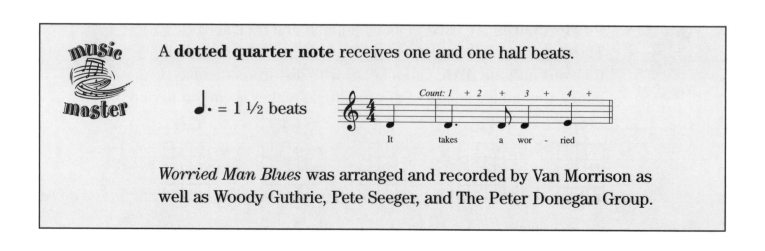

A **dotted quarter note** receives one and one half beats.

Worried Man Blues was arranged and recorded by Van Morrison as well as Woody Guthrie, Pete Seeger, and The Peter Donegan Group.

G1044

Are You Lonesome Tonight?

Music and Lyrics by
Roy Turk and Lou Handman

 Are You Lonesome Tonight? was a Billboard Hot 100 No. 1 hit for Elvis Presley in 1960.

The **flat** symbol (♭) *lowers* the pitch of a note by one fret (one half step).

G1044

Scarborough Fair

Traditional

Scarborough was an important port in medieval England. Every autumn, a large fair with merchants and musicians was held at Scarborough. The lyrics relate the story of a young man who tells a hopeful young maiden that he will take her back only if she can complete certain impossible tasks.

A version of this song was used in the movie *The Graduate*.

G1044

College Fight Song

Yale University Fight Song

College Fight Song was originally known as *Boola, Boola,* a song written in 1900 for the Yale-Harvard football game. It still remains one of the best known and often imitated of all college football fight songs.

Bill Bailey, Won't You Please Come Home?

Music and Lyrics by
Hughie Cannon

G1044

The House of the Rising Sun

Traditional

In 1964, a version of *The House of the Rising Sun* was a No. 1 hit by the English rock band The Animals. It is still regularly performed today.

G1044

I Don't Want to Wait

Philip Groeber

D.S. % al Coda ⊕—A repeat that means to go back to the sign (%) and then proceed to the **To Coda** (⊕) symbol. Then go directly to the **Coda**, which is the ending section.

The **marcato** symbol (>) near the notehead means to play the note with emphasis.

G1044

The Sound of Silence

from the movie *The Graduate*

Music and Lyrics by
Paul Simon

G1044

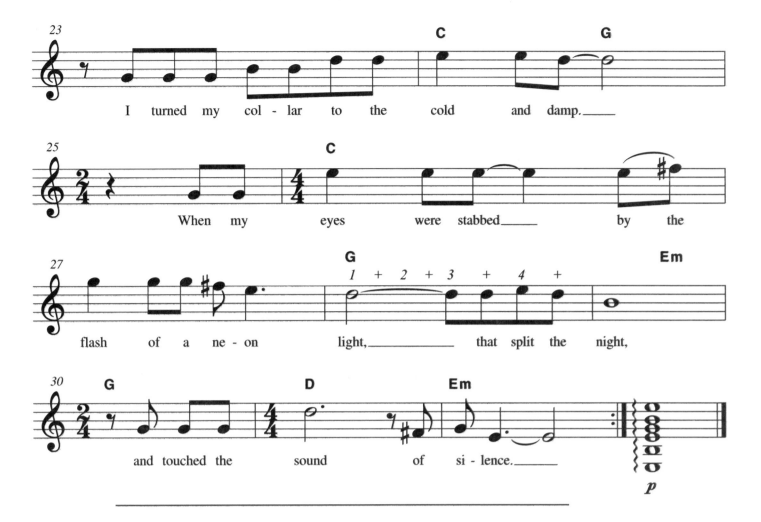

I turned my col - lar to the cold and damp.____

When my eyes were stabbed____ by the

flash of a ne - on light,_____ that split the night,

and touched the sound of si - lence.____

p

---

3. And in the naked light I saw, Ten thousand people, maybe more,
People talking without speaking, People hearing without listening.
People writing songs that voices never share, and no one dared,
Disturb the sound of silence.

4. "Fools!" said I, "You do not know, Silence like a cancer grows.
Hear my words that I might teach you, Take my arms that I might reach you."
But my words like silent raindrops fell,
And echoed in the wells of silence.

5. And the people bowed and prayed, to the neon god they made.
And the sign flashed out its warning, In the words that it was forming.
And the sign said "The words of the prophets are written on the subway walls,
and tenement halls." And whisper'd in the sound of silence.

---

*Two or more different notes may be connected by a curved line called a **slur**, not to be confused with a tie. When the second note is a higher pitch than the first, use a **hammer-on**. Play the first note, and then have the left-hand finger drop (like a hammer) to sound the second note.*

The Sound of Silence alternates between two different time signatures ($\frac{4}{4}$ and $\frac{2}{4}$). Be sure to keep the quarter notes at a steady pulse.

An **eighth rest** (♪) receives one half of a beat of silence.

Natural Notes in First Position

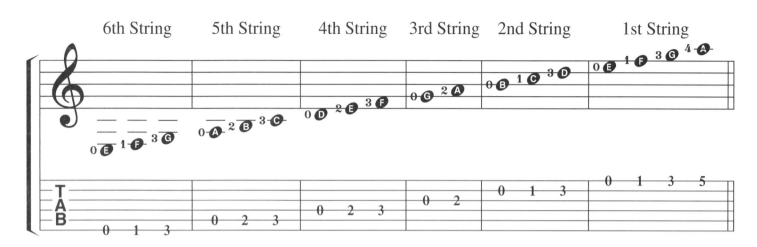

The **sharp** symbol (♯) raises the pitch of a note by one fret (one half step).

The **flat** symbol (♭) lowers the pitch of a note by one fret (one half step).

Everybody's Popular Guitar Riffs

Here are several fun-to-play riffs to get you ready for
Everybody's Popular Music for Guitar 2!

Blues Riff - Fifth Position

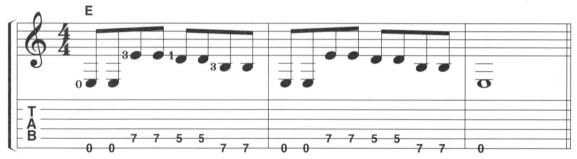

Boogie Riff - Second Position

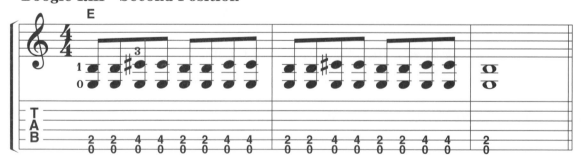

Power Chords - Changing Positions

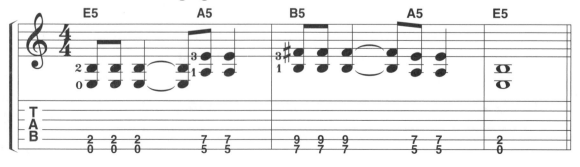

G1044

Chords Used in This Book

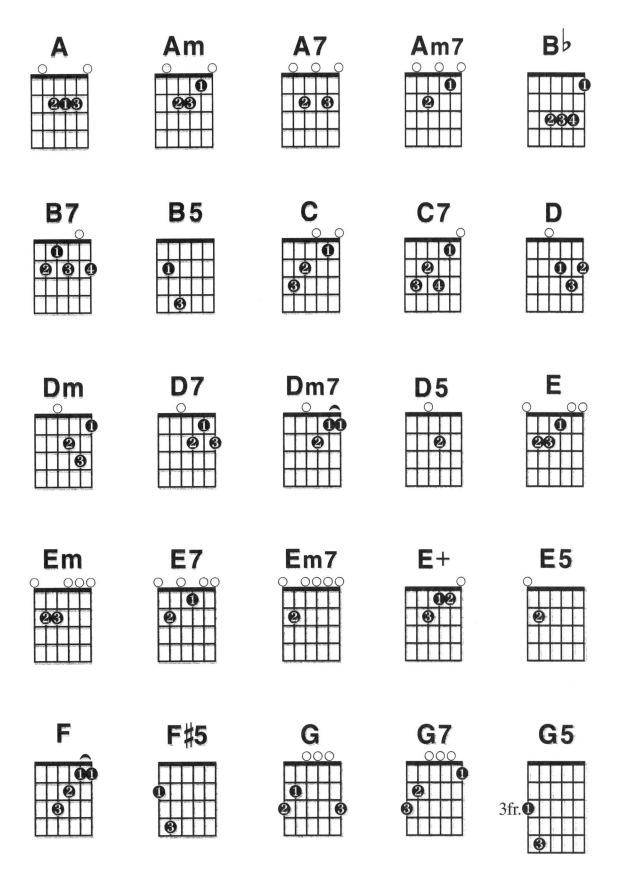

Glossary

SIGN	TERM	DEFINITION
	arpeggio	The notes of a chord played one after the other, instead of at the same time. (pg. 33)
	Bridge:	A contrasting section of a song that occurs after the verses. (pg. 20)
	Chorus:	The main section of a song that usually contains the name of the song in the lyrics. (pg. 8)
	dampen	To mute the strings, keeping them from vibrating, as during a rest. (pg. 6)
	D.S. % al Coda ⊕	Repeat from the sign (%) and end with the *Coda* (⊕). (pg. 30)
⊓	**downstroke**	Strumming downward, toward the floor. (pg. 12)
⌒	*fermata*	Indicates that a note or rest should be held longer than usual. (pg. 29)
	guide fingers	Keeping the left-hand fingers in gentle contact with a string when changing chords. (pg. 23)
	hammer-on	Play the first note. A left-hand finger then drops (like a hammer) to sound the second note. The two notes are connected by a slur. (pg. 32)
	Intro:	An introduction to a song. (pg. 29)
	Let ring	Allow the strings to vibrate as long as possible. (pg. 21)
	lyrics	The words to a song. (pg. 5)
N.C.	**No Chord**	No chords are to be played. (pg. 30)
1 2 3 4 ① ② ③ ④ ⑤ ⑥	**numbers**	2 indicates to use the second finger of the left hand; ② indicates to play on the second string. (pg. 6, 22)
	position	Assigning consecutive left-hand fingers to consecutive frets. (pg. 34)
‖: :‖	**repeat signs**	The section of music between these signs should be played again. (pg. 5)
	riff	A repeated series of notes that has an appealing sound. (pg. 34)
	ritard.	Gradually getting slower. (pg. 21)
	tablature	A notation system consisting of six horizontal lines representing the strings. The numbers placed on these lines indicate the fret on which to play. (pg. 34)
	tie	A curved line connecting notes of the same pitch. The second note is not played again with the pick but continues to sound. (pg. 5)
V	**upstroke**	Strumming upward, toward the ceiling. (pg. 12)
	Verse:	The lyrics to a song that change. (pg. 8)

G1044